The Myth of Canada Becoming the 51st State

By Mike Bhangu

BBP

Copyright 2025

Copyright © 2025 by Mike Bhangu.

This book is licensed and is being offered for your personal enjoyment only. It is prohibited for this book to be re-sold, shared and/or to be given away to other people. If you would like to provide and/or share this book with someone else, please purchase an additional copy. If you did not personally purchase this book for your own personal enjoyment and are reading it, please respect the hard work of this author and purchase a copy for yourself.

All rights reserved. No part of this book may be used or reproduced or transmitted in any manner whatsoever without written permission from the author, except for the inclusion of brief quotations in reviews, articles, and recommendations. Thank you for honoring this.

_____

Published by BB Productions
British Columbia, Canada
thinkingmanmike@gmail.com

Table of Contents

TABLE OF CONTENTS

OVERVIEW

INTRODUCTION: THE MYTH OF THE 51ST STATE

CHAPTER 1: FROM COLONY TO CONFEDERATION

CHAPTER 2: LOYALIST ROOTS AND THE AMERICAN REVOLUTION

CHAPTER 3: THE BRITISH EMPIRE AND CANADA'S PATH TO SOVEREIGNTY

CHAPTER 4: A MOSAIC, NOT A MELTING POT

CHAPTER 5: THE QUIET PATRIOTISM OF CANADIANS

CHAPTER 6: THE QUEBEC FACTOR

CHAPTER 7: ECONOMIC INDEPENDENCE AND INTEGRATION

CHAPTER 8: POLITICAL SOVEREIGNTY AND GOVERNANCE

CHAPTER 9: DEFENSE AND SECURITY

CHAPTER 10: THE LEGACY OF THE BRITISH EMPIRE

CHAPTER 11: THE COMMONWEALTH CONNECTION

CHAPTER 12: CANADA ON THE WORLD STAGE

CHAPTER 13: THE MYTH OF ANNEXATION

CHAPTER 14: STRENGTHENING CANADIAN IDENTITY IN THE 21ST CENTURY

CHAPTER 15: CONCLUSION: A SOVEREIGN FUTURE

APPENDICES

Overview

Introduction: The Myth of the 51st State

- Brief overview of the persistent speculation about Canada joining the United States.
- The importance of understanding Canada's unique identity and historical trajectory.
- Thesis: Canada's distinct national identity, historical ties to the British Empire, and contemporary global relationships make it unlikely to ever become part of the United States.

Chapter 1: From Colony to Confederation

- The evolution of Canada from a collection of British colonies to a self-governing dominion.
- The role of the British North America Act (1867) in establishing Canada as a federation.
- The War of 1812 and its impact on Canadian identity as distinct from the United States.

Chapter 2: Loyalist Roots and the American Revolution

- The migration of United Empire Loyalists to Canada after the American Revolution.
- How Loyalist values shaped Canada's political and cultural identity.
- The contrast between Canada's gradual evolution toward independence and the United States' revolutionary break from Britain.

Chapter 3: The British Empire and Canada's Path to Sovereignty

- Canada's role within the British Empire and its gradual move toward full sovereignty.

- The Statute of Westminster (1931) and its significance in granting Canada legislative independence.

- The enduring symbolic role of the British monarchy in Canada's constitutional framework.

Chapter 4: A Mosaic, Not a Melting Pot

- Canada's multiculturalism as a defining feature of its national identity.

- Contrasts with the American "melting pot" ideal and the implications for national unity.

- The role of bilingualism (English and French) in shaping Canada's unique identity.

Chapter 5: The Quiet Patriotism of Canadians

- Exploring Canadian values such as peacekeeping, moderation, and social welfare.

- The role of institutions like universal healthcare in fostering national pride.

- Why Canadians are resistant to assimilation into the American political and cultural sphere.

Chapter 6: The Quebec Factor

- The historical and ongoing significance of Quebec in Canada's federal structure.

- Quebec's distinct cultural identity and its resistance to both American and Anglo-Canadian dominance.
- How Quebec's presence complicates any hypothetical merger with the United States.

Chapter 7: Economic Independence and Integration

- The deep economic ties between Canada and the United States through trade (e.g., NAFTA, USMCA).
- Why economic integration does not equate to political integration.
- Canada's efforts to diversify its trade relationships to reduce reliance on the U.S.

Chapter 8: Political Sovereignty and Governance

- The differences between Canada's parliamentary system and the U.S. presidential system.
- Canada's commitment to multilateralism and its role in international organizations.
- The challenges of reconciling two vastly different political systems.

Chapter 9: Defense and Security

- Canada's participation in NATO and its defense relationship with the United States.
- The importance of maintaining an independent foreign policy.
- Historical examples of Canada asserting its sovereignty in opposition to U.S. interests.

Chapter 10: The Legacy of the British Empire

- The enduring influence of British legal, political, and cultural traditions in Canada.

- The role of the Crown in Canada's constitutional monarchy.

- How Canada's British heritage differentiates it from the United States.

Chapter 11: The Commonwealth Connection

- Canada's active role in the Commonwealth of Nations.

- The symbolic and practical benefits of Commonwealth membership.

- How the Commonwealth reinforces Canada's global identity separate from the United States.

Chapter 12: Canada on the World Stage

- Canada's reputation as a middle power and peacekeeper.

- Its independent stance on international issues, such as the Vietnam War and the Iraq War.

- The importance of maintaining a distinct voice in global affairs.

Chapter 13: The Myth of Annexation

- Debunking the idea that Canada would ever willingly join the United States.

- The logistical, cultural, and political barriers to such a merger.

- Public opinion in Canada and the United States on the issue.

Chapter 14: Strengthening Canadian Identity in the 21st Century

- The role of education, media, and cultural institutions in fostering national pride.

- The challenges of globalization and digital media to Canadian identity.

- Strategies for preserving and enhancing Canada's sovereignty.

Chapter 15: Conclusion: A Sovereign Future

- Recap of the key reasons Canada will remain independent.

- The importance of Canada's unique identity in a globalized world.

- A call to celebrate and protect Canada's sovereignty for future generations.

Appendices

- Timeline of key events in Canadian history.

- Selected quotes from Canadian leaders on independence and sovereignty.

Introduction: The Myth of the 51st State

The idea of Canada becoming the 51st state of the United States is a notion that has persisted for decades, often surfacing in casual conversations, political debates, and even popular culture. It is a concept that seems to capture the imagination of some Americans and Canadians alike, fueled by the two nations' geographic proximity, deep economic ties, and shared language (for the majority of Canadians). Yet, despite these connections, the idea of Canada joining the United States remains a myth—one that overlooks the profound historical, cultural, political, and social differences that define Canada as a sovereign nation. This book seeks to explore why Canada will not, and indeed cannot, become the 51st state of the United States, while also examining the unique relationship Canada has maintained with the British Empire and the Commonwealth.

At first glance, the idea of Canada merging with the United States might seem plausible. The two countries share the longest undefended border in the world, and their economies are deeply intertwined through trade agreements like the United States-Mexico-Canada Agreement (USMCA). Millions of Canadians live and work in the United States, and American culture—from Hollywood movies to fast food chains—permeates Canadian society. Yet, these surface-level connections mask a deeper truth: Canada is a nation with its own distinct identity, shaped by a history that diverges sharply from that of its southern neighbor.

Canada's journey to nationhood was not marked by a violent revolution, as was the case in the United States, but rather by a gradual evolution toward independence within the framework of the British Empire. This historical path has left an indelible mark on Canada's political institutions, cultural values, and national identity. From its origins as a collection of British colonies to its current status as a constitutional monarchy with Queen Elizabeth II (and now King Charles III) as its head of state, Canada has maintained a unique relationship with the British Crown—one that continues to shape its sense of self.

Moreover, Canada's identity is deeply rooted in its commitment to multiculturalism, bilingualism, and social welfare—values that set it apart from the United States. While the U.S. has long embraced the idea of the "melting pot," where diverse cultures are assimilated into a single national identity, Canada has chosen a different path. The Canadian mosaic celebrates diversity, allowing individuals to maintain their cultural heritage while contributing to the broader national fabric. This approach has fostered a society that prides itself on inclusivity and tolerance, further distinguishing Canada from its American neighbor.

Politically, Canada's parliamentary system and commitment to multilateralism stand in stark contrast to the U.S. presidential system and its often unilateral approach to global affairs. Canada's role as a peacekeeper and mediator on the world stage has earned it a reputation as a "middle power"—a nation that punches above its weight in international diplomacy. This independent stance has allowed Canada to carve out a unique position in global politics, one that would be impossible to maintain if it were absorbed into the United States.

Economically, while Canada and the United States are deeply interconnected, this relationship is one of partnership, not subordination. Canada has worked diligently to diversify its trade relationships, reducing its reliance on the U.S. market and strengthening ties with other nations. This economic independence is a key pillar of Canada's sovereignty, ensuring that it remains a distinct and self-determining nation.

Finally, Canada's ties to the Commonwealth of Nations—a voluntary association of countries with historical links to the British Empire—further underscore its unique place in the world. The Commonwealth provides Canada with a platform to engage with other nations on issues of mutual concern, from climate change to human rights, while also reinforcing its historical and cultural connections to the United Kingdom and other member states.

In this book, we will delve into these themes in greater detail, exploring the historical, cultural, political, and economic factors that have shaped Canada's identity and ensured its continued independence. We will examine Canada's relationship with the British Empire and the Commonwealth, its evolving role on the global stage, and the enduring values that define what it means to be Canadian. Through this exploration, we will demonstrate why the idea of Canada becoming the 51st state is not only unlikely but fundamentally at odds with the nation's history, identity, and aspirations.

The story of Canada is one of resilience, adaptability, and quiet determination. It is a story that deserves to be told in its own right, free from the shadow of its larger neighbor to the south. By understanding the forces that have shaped Canada's past and present, we can better appreciate why it will continue to chart its own course in the future—a future that does not include becoming the 51st state of the United States.

Chapter 1: From Colony to Confederation

Canada's journey from a collection of British colonies to a self-governing dominion is a story of gradual evolution, marked by compromise, negotiation, and a steadfast commitment to maintaining a distinct identity. Unlike the United States, which achieved independence through a revolutionary war, Canada's path to nationhood was characterized by a series of incremental steps, each reinforcing its ties to the British Empire while laying the groundwork for eventual sovereignty. This chapter explores the key events and decisions that shaped Canada's early history, highlighting how its unique trajectory set it apart from its southern neighbor and laid the foundation for its modern identity.

The Roots of British North America

Canada's colonial history begins long before Confederation in 1867. The territory that would become Canada was initially home to Indigenous peoples, whose societies and cultures had flourished for thousands of years. European colonization began in earnest in the 16th and 17th centuries, with the French establishing settlements in what is now Quebec and the Atlantic provinces. The British, however, soon emerged as the dominant colonial power, particularly after the Seven Years' War (1756–1763), which ended with France ceding most of its North American territories to Britain under the Treaty of Paris.

The British inherited a culturally and linguistically divided territory, with French-speaking Catholics in Quebec and English-speaking Protestants in the Atlantic colonies. To manage this diversity, the British government passed the Quebec Act of 1774, which granted French Canadians the right to practice their religion and retain their legal system. This early recognition of cultural differences would become a hallmark of Canadian governance, setting the stage for the nation's later commitment to bilingualism and multiculturalism.

The Impact of the American Revolution

The American Revolution (1775–1783) had a profound impact on Canada's development. During and after the war, tens of thousands of Loyalists—colonists who remained loyal to the British Crown—fled the newly independent United States and settled in British North America. These Loyalists brought with them a deep-seated distrust of American republicanism and a strong attachment to British institutions. Their arrival not only bolstered the population of the British colonies but also reinforced a distinct Canadian identity rooted in loyalty to the Crown and a preference for gradual, peaceful change over revolution.

The influx of Loyalists also led to the division of Quebec into two colonies: Upper Canada (modern-day Ontario) and Lower Canada (modern-day Quebec). This division was formalized in the Constitutional Act of 1791, which established representative governments in both colonies while maintaining British control over key decisions. Although these governments were far from fully democratic, they marked an important step toward self-governance.

The Road to Confederation

By the mid-19th century, the British North American colonies faced a series of challenges that prompted them to consider unification. Economic pressures, such as the loss of preferential trade agreements with Britain, highlighted the need for a more integrated economy. Politically, the colonies were struggling with deadlock and instability, particularly in the Province of Canada (which included Upper and Lower Canada). Externally, the threat of American expansionism, exemplified by the Manifest Destiny ideology and the Fenian raids, underscored the importance of collective defense.

These challenges culminated in a series of conferences—most notably the Charlottetown Conference (1864) and the Quebec Conference (1864)—where leaders from the colonies discussed the possibility of forming a federation. The result was the British North America Act (BNA Act) of 1867, which united the colonies of Ontario, Quebec, New Brunswick, and Nova Scotia into the Dominion of Canada. The BNA Act established a federal system of government, dividing powers between the federal and provincial levels, and laid the foundation for Canada's constitutional framework.

Confederation and Its Significance

Confederation was a landmark moment in Canadian history, marking the birth of a new nation within the British Empire. While Canada remained a British dominion, the BNA Act granted it a significant degree of self-governance, particularly in domestic affairs. The new federal structure allowed for the accommodation of regional differences, particularly between English-speaking and French-speaking Canadians, and set the stage for the eventual inclusion of other provinces and territories.

Confederation also reflected Canada's unique approach to nation-building. Unlike the United States, which had declared independence through a revolutionary war, Canada achieved self-governance through negotiation and compromise, with the blessing of the British Crown. This approach reinforced Canada's identity as a nation that valued stability, continuity, and peaceful evolution over radical change.

The Legacy of Early Canadian History
The events leading up to Confederation left a lasting imprint on Canada's national identity. The emphasis on compromise and accommodation, the recognition of cultural and linguistic diversity, and the commitment to gradual change all became defining features of Canadian society. These values set Canada apart from the United States and laid the groundwork for its future development as a sovereign nation.

Moreover, Canada's early history underscores the importance of its relationship with the British Empire. While the United States rejected British rule, Canada embraced its British heritage, using it as a foundation for building a distinct national identity. This relationship would continue to evolve in the decades following Confederation, as Canada gradually asserted its independence while maintaining ties to the Crown and the Commonwealth.

In conclusion, the story of Canada's journey from colony to Confederation is one of resilience, adaptability, and quiet determination. It is a story that highlights the nation's unique approach to nation-building and its commitment to preserving its distinct identity. By understanding this history, we can better appreciate why Canada has remained a sovereign nation—and why it will continue to do so in the future.

The Myth of Canada Becoming the 51st State

Chapter 2: Loyalist Roots and the American Revolution

The American Revolution (1775–1783) was a transformative event not only for the fledgling United States but also for the British colonies to the north that would eventually become Canada. While the Revolution gave birth to the United States, it also solidified the identity of British North America as a distinct entity, shaped by the values and experiences of those who remained loyal to the British Crown. This chapter explores the profound impact of the American Revolution on Canada's development, focusing on the migration of United Empire Loyalists, the cultural and political legacy they left behind, and how their experiences set Canada on a path fundamentally different from that of the United States.

The Loyalists: Who Were They?
The United Empire Loyalists were American colonists who remained loyal to the British Crown during the American Revolution. Their reasons for loyalty varied: some were motivated by principle, believing in the legitimacy of British rule; others were driven by practical considerations, such as economic ties to Britain or fear of the social upheaval that independence might bring. Regardless of their motivations, the Loyalists found themselves on the losing side of the Revolution, facing persecution, confiscation of property, and even violence from their revolutionary neighbors.

When the war ended with the Treaty of Paris in 1783, tens of thousands of Loyalists fled the newly independent United States. Many sought refuge in the remaining British colonies to the north, particularly in Nova Scotia, Quebec, and the unsettled lands that would later become Ontario. This mass migration had a profound impact on the demographic, cultural, and political landscape of British North America.

The Loyalist Migration and Its Impact

The arrival of the Loyalists in British North America marked a turning point in the region's history. In Nova Scotia, the influx of Loyalists was so significant that it led to the creation of a new colony: New Brunswick, established in 1784 to accommodate the growing population. In Quebec, the Loyalists settled primarily in the western part of the colony, which was eventually separated to form Upper Canada (modern-day Ontario) in 1791.

The Loyalists brought with them not only their loyalty to the British Crown but also their cultural and political values. Many were educated, middle-class individuals who had been influential in their former communities. They established schools, churches, and newspapers, laying the groundwork for a vibrant civil society. Their commitment to British institutions, such as parliamentary governance and the rule of law, helped shape the political culture of British North America.

Loyalist Values and Canadian Identity

The Loyalists' experiences during and after the Revolution had a lasting impact on Canadian identity. Having witnessed the upheaval and violence of the Revolution, they were deeply skeptical of republicanism and radical change. Instead, they valued stability, order, and gradual reform—values that would come to define Canada's political culture.

This emphasis on continuity and loyalty to the Crown set Canada apart from the United States, which had embraced revolutionary ideals of liberty, equality, and self-governance. While the United States celebrated its break from Britain as a triumph of democracy, Canada prided itself on its peaceful evolution within the British Empire. This distinction became a cornerstone of Canadian identity, reinforcing the notion that Canada was a distinct nation with its own values and traditions.

The Constitutional Act of 1791
The Loyalist migration also had significant political implications. To accommodate the growing English-speaking population in Quebec, the British government passed the Constitutional Act of 1791, which divided the colony into Upper Canada (Ontario) and Lower Canada (Quebec). Each colony was granted a representative assembly, though ultimate authority remained in the hands of the British-appointed governor.

The Constitutional Act reflected the Loyalists' desire for British institutions, such as elected assemblies and English common law, while also recognizing the distinct cultural and legal traditions of French-speaking Canadians in Lower Canada. This balancing act between English and French interests would become a defining feature of Canadian governance, setting the stage for the nation's later commitment to bilingualism and federalism.

The War of 1812 and the Reinforcement of Loyalist Identity

The War of 1812 between the United States and Britain further reinforced the Loyalist legacy in Canada. During the war, American forces attempted to invade British North America, hoping to annex the colonies and fulfill the ideology of Manifest Destiny. However, the invasion was repelled, thanks in part to the efforts of Canadian militias and Indigenous allies.

The War of 1812 became a defining moment in Canadian history, symbolizing the colony's determination to resist American expansionism and maintain its ties to Britain. For the descendants of the Loyalists, the war was a validation of their decision to remain loyal to the Crown and a reminder of the dangers posed by American republicanism.

The Legacy of the Loyalists

The Loyalists' influence on Canada's development cannot be overstated. Their migration transformed the demographic and cultural landscape of British North America, laying the foundation for the nation that would emerge in the 19th and 20th centuries. Their values—loyalty to the Crown, a preference for gradual change, and a commitment to stability and order—became deeply embedded in Canadian identity.

Moreover, the Loyalists' experiences set Canada on a path fundamentally different from that of the United States. While the U.S. embraced revolution and republicanism, Canada chose a path of evolution and continuity within the British Empire. This distinction remains a key factor in understanding why Canada has maintained its independence and why the idea of it becoming the 51st state is so far-fetched.

In conclusion, the story of the Loyalists is a testament to the resilience and determination of those who shaped Canada's early history. Their legacy lives on in the nation's institutions, values, and identity, serving as a reminder of why Canada remains a distinct and sovereign nation. By understanding the Loyalist roots of Canadian identity, we can better appreciate the forces that have shaped the nation's past and continue to guide its future.

The Myth of Canada Becoming the 51st State

Chapter 3: The British Empire and Canada's Path to Sovereignty

Canada's relationship with the British Empire is a cornerstone of its national identity and historical development. Unlike the United States, which severed its ties with Britain through revolution, Canada's journey to sovereignty was marked by a gradual and peaceful evolution within the framework of the British Empire. This chapter explores how Canada's ties to the British Empire shaped its political institutions, cultural identity, and path to independence, ultimately setting it apart from its southern neighbor and reinforcing its status as a distinct nation.

Canada's Role in the British Empire

From the early days of British colonization, Canada was an integral part of the British Empire. As a collection of colonies, it provided raw materials, such as timber and fur, to fuel Britain's industrial economy. In return, Britain offered military protection, economic investment, and a sense of belonging to a global empire. This relationship was mutually beneficial, but it also placed Canada in a subordinate position, with key decisions being made in London rather than in the colonies themselves.

Despite this subordination, Canada's role within the Empire was unique. Unlike other colonies, which were often governed directly by British officials, Canada was granted a degree of self-governance through representative assemblies. This early experience with self-rule laid the groundwork for Canada's eventual transition to full sovereignty.

The Durham Report and Responsible Government

One of the most significant milestones in Canada's path to sovereignty was the Durham Report of 1839. Following the rebellions of 1837–1838 in Upper and Lower Canada, Britain sent Lord Durham to investigate the causes of the unrest. Durham's report recommended the unification of Upper and Lower Canada and the introduction of responsible government—a system in which the executive branch is accountable to the elected legislature rather than to the British Crown.

Although Durham's recommendations were initially met with resistance, they eventually led to the Act of Union of 1841, which united Upper and Lower Canada into the Province of Canada. More importantly, the concept of responsible government became a cornerstone of Canadian political development. By the mid-19th century, Canada had achieved responsible government, marking a significant step toward self-rule.

Confederation and the Birth of the Dominion

The next major step in Canada's path to sovereignty was Confederation in 1867. The British North America Act (BNA Act) united the colonies of Ontario, Quebec, New Brunswick, and Nova Scotia into the Dominion of Canada, creating a federal system of government with a strong central authority. While the BNA Act granted Canada a significant degree of self-governance, it also maintained ties to the British Empire, particularly in areas such as foreign policy and defense.

Confederation was a pragmatic response to the challenges facing British North America, including economic instability, political deadlock, and the threat of American expansionism. By uniting the colonies, Canada was able to strengthen its economy, streamline its governance, and present a united front against external threats. At the same time, Confederation reinforced Canada's ties to Britain, ensuring that it remained part of the Empire while gradually asserting its independence.

The Statute of Westminster and Legislative Independence
Canada's journey to full sovereignty reached a critical milestone with the Statute of Westminster of 1931. This legislation, passed by the British Parliament, granted Canada and other dominions (such as Australia and New Zealand) full legislative independence. No longer was Canada subject to British laws or oversight; it was free to make its own decisions in all areas, including foreign policy and defense.

The Statute of Westminster was a recognition of Canada's growing maturity as a nation. By the early 20th century, Canada had proven its ability to govern itself, both domestically and internationally. Its contributions to World War I, particularly at battles such as Vimy Ridge, had demonstrated its commitment to the Empire while also asserting its distinct identity. The Statute of Westminster formalized this reality, marking Canada's transition from a dominion to a fully sovereign nation.

The Role of the Monarchy in Canadian Identity
Even as Canada achieved legislative independence, it maintained its ties to the British Crown. The monarchy remains a central symbol of

Canadian identity, representing continuity, tradition, and the rule of law. While the role of the monarch is largely ceremonial, it serves as a reminder of Canada's historical ties to Britain and its unique path to sovereignty.

The monarchy also plays a unifying role in Canada's federal system. As the head of state, the monarch represents all Canadians, regardless of their province or territory. This symbolic role helps to balance the diverse regional and cultural interests within Canada, reinforcing the nation's commitment to unity and inclusivity.

Canada's Evolving Relationship with the Commonwealth
Canada's ties to the British Empire have evolved into a modern relationship with the Commonwealth of Nations. The Commonwealth, a voluntary association of countries with historical links to Britain, provides Canada with a platform to engage with other nations on issues of mutual concern, from trade to climate change. While the Commonwealth no longer holds the same political significance as the British Empire, it remains an important symbol of Canada's historical and cultural connections to Britain and the wider world.

The Legacy of the British Empire
Canada's relationship with the British Empire has left a lasting imprint on its national identity. The values of stability, continuity, and gradual reform that characterized Canada's path to sovereignty remain central to its political culture. At the same time, Canada's ability to assert its

independence within the framework of the Empire demonstrates its resilience and adaptability.

This legacy sets Canada apart from the United States, which achieved independence through revolution and rejection of British rule. While the U.S. embraced a radical break with its colonial past, Canada chose a path of evolution and continuity, maintaining its ties to Britain while gradually asserting its sovereignty. This distinction remains a key factor in understanding why Canada has maintained its independence and why the idea of it becoming the 51st state is so far-fetched.

In conclusion, Canada's path to sovereignty within the British Empire is a testament to its unique approach to nation-building. By understanding this history, we can better appreciate the forces that have shaped Canada's identity and ensured its continued independence. The story of Canada's relationship with the British Empire is one of resilience, adaptability, and quiet determination—a story that continues to define the nation today.

Chapter 4: A Mosaic, Not a Melting Pot

Canada's approach to diversity and multiculturalism is one of its defining characteristics, setting it apart from many other nations, particularly its southern neighbor, the United States. While the U.S. has long embraced the idea of the "melting pot," where diverse cultures are assimilated into a single national identity, Canada has chosen a different path. The Canadian mosaic celebrates diversity, allowing individuals to maintain their cultural heritage while contributing to the broader national fabric. This chapter explores the origins, development, and significance of Canada's multicultural identity, highlighting how it has shaped the nation's social, cultural, and political landscape.

The Origins of Multiculturalism in Canada

Canada's multicultural identity has deep historical roots, dating back to its earliest days as a colony. The presence of Indigenous peoples, French settlers, and British colonists created a diverse society from the outset. The Quebec Act of 1774, which recognized the rights of French Canadians to practice their religion and retain their legal system, was an early acknowledgment of this diversity. Similarly, the Constitutional Act of 1791, which divided Quebec into Upper Canada (English-speaking) and Lower Canada (French-speaking), reflected the need to accommodate different cultural and linguistic groups.

The arrival of United Empire Loyalists after the American Revolution further enriched Canada's cultural landscape, bringing with them a commitment to British institutions and values. Over time, waves of immigrants from Europe, Asia, Africa, and other parts of the world added to this diversity, making Canada one of the most multicultural nations on earth.

The Official Policy of Multiculturalism

Canada's commitment to multiculturalism was formally recognized in 1971, when Prime Minister Pierre Trudeau announced the adoption of an official policy of multiculturalism. This policy was a response to the growing diversity of Canadian society and the need to address issues of discrimination and inequality. It affirmed the value of cultural diversity and committed the government to promoting the full and equitable participation of all Canadians, regardless of their cultural background.

The policy of multiculturalism was later enshrined in law with the Canadian Multiculturalism Act of 1988. This legislation reaffirmed Canada's commitment to preserving and enhancing multiculturalism, recognizing it as a fundamental characteristic of Canadian identity. The Act also mandated the government to promote understanding and respect for diversity, combat racism and discrimination, and support the cultural expression of all Canadians.

The Canadian Mosaic in Practice

The concept of the Canadian mosaic is evident in many aspects of Canadian life. In cities like Toronto, Vancouver, and Montreal, neighborhoods are home to vibrant cultural communities, each contributing to the richness of Canadian society. Festivals, such as Caribana in Toronto and the Montreal International Jazz Festival, celebrate this diversity, bringing together people from different backgrounds to share in each other's traditions and customs.

Canada's education system also reflects its commitment to multiculturalism. Schools across the country teach students about the contributions of different cultural groups to Canadian society, fostering an appreciation for diversity from a young age. Language programs, such as French immersion and heritage language classes, allow students to maintain and develop their linguistic and cultural heritage.

Multiculturalism and National Identity
Multiculturalism is not just a policy in Canada; it is a core part of the national identity. Canadians take pride in their country's diversity and its reputation as a welcoming and inclusive society. This pride is reflected in the national motto, "A Mari Usque Ad Mare" ("From Sea to Sea"), which symbolizes the vastness and diversity of the country.

The Canadian mosaic also sets Canada apart from the United States, where the "melting pot" ideal has often led to the assimilation of immigrant cultures into a dominant American identity. In contrast, Canada's approach allows for the coexistence of multiple identities, creating a society that is both diverse and unified. This distinction is a source of pride for Canadians and a key factor in the nation's ability to attract immigrants from around the world.

Challenges and Criticisms of Multiculturalism

While Canada's multiculturalism policy has been largely successful, it is not without its challenges and criticisms. Some argue that multiculturalism can lead to the fragmentation of society, with different cultural groups living in isolation from one another. Others contend that the policy has not gone far enough in addressing systemic racism and inequality, particularly for Indigenous peoples and racialized communities.

In recent years, there has been a growing recognition of the need to reconcile multiculturalism with the rights and aspirations of Indigenous peoples. The Truth and Reconciliation Commission (2015) and the National Inquiry into Missing and Murdered Indigenous Women and Girls (2019) have highlighted the ongoing impacts of colonialism and the need for a more inclusive and equitable approach to diversity.

The Future of Multiculturalism in Canada

Despite these challenges, multiculturalism remains a cornerstone of Canadian identity. As Canada continues to welcome immigrants from around the world, the mosaic will only grow richer and more complex. The challenge for Canada will be to ensure that all cultural groups, including Indigenous peoples, are able to fully participate in and contribute to Canadian society.

This will require ongoing efforts to combat racism and discrimination, promote understanding and respect, and address the systemic barriers that prevent some groups from achieving their full potential. It will also require a commitment to reconciliation with Indigenous peoples, recognizing their unique status and rights as the original inhabitants of the land.

Conclusion: The Strength of Diversity
Canada's multicultural identity is one of its greatest strengths, setting it apart from other nations and contributing to its reputation as a welcoming and inclusive society. The Canadian mosaic is a testament to the nation's ability to embrace diversity and build a society that is both unified and diverse. By understanding the origins, development, and significance of multiculturalism in Canada, we can better appreciate the forces that have shaped the nation's identity and ensured its continued success.

In a world that is increasingly interconnected and diverse, Canada's approach to multiculturalism offers a model for how nations can celebrate diversity while fostering unity. It is a model that reflects the values of inclusivity, respect, and equality—values that are at the heart of what it means to be Canadian.

Chapter 5: The Quiet Patriotism of Canadians

Canadian patriotism is often described as "quiet" or "understated," a stark contrast to the more overt and demonstrative forms of nationalism seen in other countries, particularly the United States. This chapter explores the unique nature of Canadian patriotism, examining its roots, manifestations, and significance in shaping the nation's identity. From the country's commitment to peacekeeping and social welfare to its emphasis on inclusivity and moderation, Canadian patriotism reflects a set of values that distinguish it from the more assertive nationalism of its southern neighbor.

The Roots of Quiet Patriotism

Canadian patriotism is deeply rooted in the nation's history and cultural values. Unlike the United States, which was born out of a revolutionary struggle for independence, Canada's path to nationhood was marked by gradual evolution and compromise. This historical trajectory fostered a sense of pride in stability, continuity, and peaceful change, rather than in dramatic displays of nationalistic fervor.

The influence of the United Empire Loyalists, who fled the American Revolution to remain loyal to the British Crown, also played a significant role in shaping Canadian patriotism. Their experiences instilled a deep-seated skepticism of radicalism and a preference for moderation and order. These values became embedded in the Canadian psyche, influencing the nation's approach to governance, diplomacy, and national identity.

Peacekeeping and Global Citizenship

One of the most prominent expressions of Canadian patriotism is the country's commitment to peacekeeping and multilateralism. Since the mid-20th century, Canada has played a leading role in United Nations peacekeeping missions, earning a reputation as a "middle power" that punches above its weight in international diplomacy.

The image of Canadian peacekeepers as impartial mediators and protectors of vulnerable populations has become a source of national pride. This commitment to peacekeeping reflects a broader Canadian value system that prioritizes cooperation, dialogue, and the peaceful resolution of conflicts. It also underscores Canada's belief in the importance of contributing to global stability and security, rather than pursuing unilateral or aggressive foreign policies.

Social Welfare and the Common Good

Another key aspect of Canadian patriotism is the nation's commitment to social welfare and the common good. Programs such as universal healthcare, public education, and social safety nets are seen as fundamental expressions of Canadian values, reflecting a belief in the importance of collective responsibility and equity.

The Canadian healthcare system, in particular, is a source of immense national pride. Often cited as a defining feature of Canadian identity, it embodies the principle that access to healthcare is a right, not a privilege. This commitment to social welfare sets Canada apart from the United

States, where healthcare and other social services are often viewed through the lens of individual responsibility and market dynamics.

Inclusivity and Multiculturalism

Canadian patriotism is also closely tied to the nation's commitment to inclusivity and multiculturalism. Unlike more exclusionary forms of nationalism, which emphasize a singular cultural or ethnic identity, Canadian patriotism celebrates diversity and the contributions of all cultural groups to the national fabric.

This inclusive approach is reflected in national symbols and celebrations. For example, Canada Day is marked by events that highlight the country's cultural diversity, with performances, foods, and traditions from around the world. Similarly, the national anthem, "O Canada," has been translated into multiple languages and is often sung in Indigenous languages at public events.

Moderation and Humility

Canadian patriotism is characterized by a sense of moderation and humility. Canadians tend to shy away from overt displays of national pride, preferring instead to express their love for their country in more subtle and understated ways. This humility is often attributed to the nation's history and geography, which have fostered a sense of modesty and resilience.

This quiet patriotism is evident in the way Canadians view their achievements and contributions. While Canadians take pride in their country's accomplishments, they are often quick to downplay their significance or attribute them to collective effort rather than individual heroism. This modesty is a defining feature of Canadian identity, setting it apart from the more boastful and individualistic forms of patriotism seen in other countries.

Challenges to Quiet Patriotism

While quiet patriotism has served Canada well, it is not without its challenges. In an increasingly globalized and interconnected world, some argue that Canada needs to adopt a more assertive and confident approach to national identity. Others contend that the country's emphasis on inclusivity and multiculturalism has come at the expense of a cohesive national identity.

In recent years, there has been a growing recognition of the need to reconcile Canadian patriotism with the rights and aspirations of Indigenous peoples. The Truth and Reconciliation Commission (2015) and the National Inquiry into Missing and Murdered Indigenous Women and Girls (2019) have highlighted the ongoing impacts of colonialism and the need for a more inclusive and equitable approach to national identity.

The Future of Canadian Patriotism

As Canada continues to evolve, so too will its expressions of patriotism. The challenge for Canadians will be to maintain the values of inclusivity, moderation, and humility that have defined their national identity, while also addressing the challenges and inequalities that persist in society.

This will require a renewed commitment to reconciliation with Indigenous peoples, as well as efforts to combat racism, discrimination, and social inequality. It will also require a recognition of the importance of global citizenship and the need to contribute to international peace and stability.

Conclusion: The Strength of Quiet Patriotism

Canadian patriotism is a reflection of the nation's values and history, embodying a commitment to peacekeeping, social welfare, inclusivity, and moderation. This quiet and understated form of patriotism sets Canada apart from other nations, contributing to its reputation as a compassionate, cooperative, and resilient society.

By understanding the roots and manifestations of Canadian patriotism, we can better appreciate the forces that have shaped the nation's identity and ensured its continued success. In a world that is increasingly divided and polarized, Canada's quiet patriotism offers a model for how nations can celebrate their achievements while remaining humble, inclusive, and committed to the common good. It is a model that reflects the values of peace, equity, and respect—values that are at the heart of what it means to be Canadian.

The Myth of Canada Becoming the 51st State

Chapter 6: The Quebec Factor

Quebec's unique cultural, linguistic, and political identity has played a pivotal role in shaping Canada's national character and its trajectory as a sovereign nation. As the only predominantly French-speaking province in a predominantly English-speaking country, Quebec has long been a focal point of Canada's efforts to balance regional and cultural diversity within a unified federal framework. This chapter explores the historical, cultural, and political dimensions of Quebec's role in Canada, highlighting how its distinct identity has influenced the nation's development and why it serves as a key reason why Canada will not become the 51st state of the United States.

The Historical Roots of Quebec's Distinct Identity
Quebec's distinct identity dates back to its founding as New France in the early 17th century. The French settlers who established Quebec brought with them their language, culture, and Catholic faith, creating a society that was fundamentally different from the English-speaking colonies to the south. Even after the British conquest of New France in 1763, Quebec retained its French character, thanks in part to the Quebec Act of 1774, which guaranteed the rights of French Canadians to practice their religion and maintain their legal system.

The arrival of United Empire Loyalists after the American Revolution further solidified Quebec's distinct identity. While the Loyalists settled primarily in what would become Ontario, their presence reinforced the cultural and linguistic divide between English-speaking and French-speaking Canadians. This divide was formalized in the Constitutional Act of 1791, which divided Quebec into Upper Canada (English-speaking) and Lower Canada (French-speaking), setting the stage for the ongoing tension between the two linguistic groups.

The Quiet Revolution and the Rise of Quebec Nationalism
The mid-20th century marked a turning point in Quebec's history with the advent of the Quiet Revolution (Révolution tranquille). During this period, Quebec underwent a profound social, cultural, and political transformation, as the province sought to modernize its economy, secularize its institutions, and assert its identity within Canada.

The Quiet Revolution gave rise to a powerful Quebec nationalist movement, which sought greater autonomy for the province and, in some cases, outright independence. This movement culminated in the election of the Parti Québécois (PQ) in 1976 and the holding of two referendums on Quebec sovereignty, in 1980 and 1995. Although both referendums resulted in votes to remain part of Canada, they underscored the depth of Quebec's distinct identity and its desire for self-determination.

Quebec's Role in Canadian Federalism
Quebec's distinct identity has had a profound impact on the structure and functioning of Canadian federalism. From the very beginning, Canada's federal system was designed to accommodate the linguistic and cultural differences between Quebec and the rest of the country. The British North America Act of 1867, which established Canada as a federation, granted

Quebec significant powers over areas such as education, language, and civil law, ensuring that the province could preserve its unique character.

Over time, Quebec's demands for greater autonomy have led to significant changes in Canada's constitutional framework. The Official Languages Act of 1969, which made English and French the official languages of Canada, was a direct response to Quebec's concerns about the preservation of French language and culture. Similarly, the Charter of Rights and Freedoms (1982) included provisions to protect minority language rights, reflecting the ongoing importance of linguistic duality in Canadian society.

Quebec's Resistance to American Influence

Quebec's distinct identity also plays a key role in Canada's resistance to American cultural and political influence. As a French-speaking society with a strong sense of cultural pride, Quebec has long been a bastion of resistance to the homogenizing forces of Americanization. This resistance is evident in Quebec's efforts to protect and promote its language, culture, and media, as well as its skepticism of free trade agreements and other forms of economic integration with the United States.

Quebec's commitment to preserving its distinct identity serves as a powerful counterbalance to the idea of Canada becoming the 51st state. For Quebecers, the prospect of joining the United States would mean not only the loss of Canadian sovereignty but also the erosion of their linguistic and cultural heritage. This deep-seated commitment to cultural preservation makes Quebec a key player in ensuring Canada's continued independence.

The Challenges of Accommodating Quebec

While Quebec's distinct identity is a source of strength for Canada, it also presents ongoing challenges. The tension between Quebec's desire for autonomy and the federal government's desire for unity has been a recurring theme in Canadian politics, leading to debates over issues such as constitutional reform, fiscal federalism, and the division of powers.

The failure of the Meech Lake Accord (1987) and the Charlottetown Accord (1992), both of which sought to address Quebec's constitutional concerns, highlights the difficulty of reconciling Quebec's aspirations with the needs of the broader federation. These failures have left a legacy of frustration and mistrust, underscoring the need for ongoing dialogue and compromise.

Quebec's Contribution to Canadian Identity

Despite these challenges, Quebec's distinct identity has made an invaluable contribution to Canadian identity. The province's rich cultural heritage, vibrant arts scene, and commitment to social justice have enriched the national fabric, making Canada a more diverse and dynamic society.

Quebec's emphasis on inclusivity and social welfare has also influenced Canadian values, contributing to the development of programs such as universal healthcare and affordable childcare. In this sense, Quebec's distinct identity is not just a challenge to be managed but a source of strength and inspiration for the entire country.

Conclusion: Quebec as a Pillar of Canadian Sovereignty
Quebec's unique cultural, linguistic, and political identity is a defining feature of Canada's national character and a key reason why the country will not become the 51st state of the United States. The province's commitment to preserving its distinct identity, its resistance to American influence, and its ongoing demands for autonomy all serve as powerful reminders of the importance of diversity and self-determination in Canadian society.

By understanding the historical, cultural, and political dimensions of Quebec's role in Canada, we can better appreciate the forces that have shaped the nation's development and ensured its continued independence. Quebec's story is one of resilience, pride, and determination—a story that reflects the broader Canadian experience and underscores the importance of celebrating and protecting the nation's diversity. In a world that is increasingly interconnected and homogenized, Quebec's distinct identity serves as a beacon of cultural preservation and national sovereignty, reminding us of the value of standing apart while remaining united.

Chapter 7: Economic Independence and Integration

Canada's economic relationship with the United States is one of the most complex and interdependent in the world. The two nations share the largest bilateral trading relationship globally, with billions of dollars in goods and services crossing the border each year. Yet, despite this deep economic integration, Canada has maintained its economic independence, carefully balancing its ties to the U.S. with efforts to diversify its trade relationships and protect its sovereignty. This chapter explores the dynamics of Canada's economic relationship with the United States, highlighting how the country has navigated the challenges of integration while preserving its autonomy.

The Foundations of Economic Integration
Canada's economic ties to the United States have deep historical roots, dating back to the colonial era. The proximity of the two nations, combined with their shared language (for the majority of Canadians) and cultural similarities, has facilitated trade and investment for centuries. However, it was in the 20th century that the economic relationship between Canada and the U.S. truly deepened, driven by factors such as industrialization, technological advancements, and the growth of multinational corporations.

The Auto Pact of 1965 marked a significant milestone in this relationship, creating a integrated North American automotive industry and setting the stage for broader economic integration. This was followed by the Canada-U.S. Free Trade Agreement (CUSFTA) in 1988 and the North American Free Trade Agreement (NAFTA) in 1994, which further liberalized trade and investment between Canada, the U.S., and Mexico. These agreements have been instrumental in shaping the modern economic relationship between Canada and the United States, creating a highly integrated North American market.

The Benefits of Economic Integration
The economic integration between Canada and the United States has brought significant benefits to both nations. For Canada, access to the vast U.S. market has been a key driver of economic growth, providing opportunities for Canadian businesses to expand and compete on a global scale. The U.S. is Canada's largest trading partner, accounting for the majority of its exports and imports. Key sectors such as energy, automotive, agriculture, and technology have thrived as a result of this integration, creating jobs and prosperity for Canadians.

For the United States, Canada is a reliable and stable trading partner, providing essential resources such as oil, natural gas, and lumber. The two nations' supply chains are deeply intertwined, particularly in industries such as automotive and aerospace, where components and finished products frequently cross the border multiple times during the production process. This integration has enhanced the competitiveness of both nations in the global economy.

The Risks of Over-Reliance on the U.S. Market

Despite the benefits of economic integration, Canada's heavy reliance on the U.S. market poses significant risks. Over-dependence on a single trading partner makes Canada vulnerable to changes in U.S. economic policy, political developments, and market conditions. For example, the election of protectionist leaders in the U.S., such as Donald Trump, has led to uncertainty and instability in the bilateral relationship, as seen in the renegotiation of NAFTA and the imposition of tariffs on Canadian steel and aluminum.

The COVID-19 pandemic further highlighted the risks of over-reliance on the U.S. market, as disruptions to cross-border trade and supply chains exposed the fragility of the integrated North American economy. These challenges have underscored the need for Canada to diversify its trade relationships and reduce its dependence on the United States.

Efforts to Diversify Trade Relationships

Recognizing the risks of over-reliance on the U.S. market, Canada has made concerted efforts to diversify its trade relationships. The country has pursued free trade agreements with a wide range of nations, including the European Union (through the Comprehensive Economic and Trade Agreement, or CETA), the Asia-Pacific region (through the Comprehensive and Progressive Agreement for Trans-Pacific Partnership, or CPTPP), and Latin America (through agreements such as the Canada-Chile Free Trade Agreement).

These agreements have opened new markets for Canadian goods and services, reducing the country's dependence on the U.S. and enhancing its economic resilience. For example, CETA has provided Canadian businesses with access to the EU's vast single market, while the CPTPP has strengthened Canada's ties to fast-growing economies in Asia.

The Role of Natural Resources

Canada's abundant natural resources, including oil, natural gas, minerals, and timber, play a crucial role in its economic independence. The country is one of the world's largest exporters of energy and natural resources, providing a stable source of revenue and economic security. However, the reliance on resource exports also presents challenges, such as environmental concerns and vulnerability to fluctuations in global commodity prices.

To address these challenges, Canada has sought to develop more sustainable and value-added industries, such as clean energy, advanced manufacturing, and technology. These efforts are aimed at reducing the country's dependence on resource exports and creating a more diversified and resilient economy.

The Impact of Economic Integration on Sovereignty

While economic integration with the United States has brought significant benefits, it has also raised concerns about Canada's ability to maintain its sovereignty. Critics argue that the deep integration of the two economies has limited Canada's ability to pursue independent economic policies, particularly in areas such as environmental regulation, labor standards, and cultural protection.

For example, provisions in trade agreements such as NAFTA and its successor, the United States-Mexico-Canada Agreement (USMCA), have been criticized for restricting Canada's ability to regulate industries such as energy and pharmaceuticals. Similarly, the dominance of U.S. media and entertainment in Canada has raised concerns about the erosion of Canadian cultural identity.

Balancing Integration and Independence
Despite these challenges, Canada has managed to balance economic integration with the United States and the preservation of its sovereignty. The country has implemented policies to protect key industries, such as cultural exemptions in trade agreements and support for Canadian content in media and entertainment. It has also pursued initiatives to strengthen its economic resilience, such as investing in infrastructure, innovation, and education.

Moreover, Canada's commitment to multilateralism and global trade has allowed it to maintain a degree of independence from the United States. By engaging with a wide range of trading partners and participating in international organizations such as the World Trade Organization (WTO), Canada has been able to diversify its economic relationships and reduce its vulnerability to U.S. influence.

Conclusion: Economic Independence in an Interconnected World

Canada's economic relationship with the United States is a testament to the benefits and challenges of deep economic integration. While the two nations' economies are deeply intertwined, Canada has managed to maintain its economic independence through careful policy choices, diversification efforts, and a commitment to sovereignty.

By understanding the dynamics of this relationship, we can better appreciate the forces that have shaped Canada's economic development and ensured its continued success. In an increasingly interconnected and globalized world, Canada's ability to balance integration and independence serves as a model for other nations seeking to navigate the complexities of the modern economy. It is a model that reflects the values of resilience, adaptability, and self-determination—values that are at the heart of what it means to be Canadian.

Chapter 8: Political Sovereignty and Governance

Canada's political system and governance structure are fundamental to its identity as a sovereign nation. Unlike the United States, which operates under a presidential system with a clear separation of powers, Canada's parliamentary system and constitutional monarchy reflect its unique historical and cultural heritage. This chapter explores the key features of Canada's political system, its evolution over time, and how it has enabled the country to maintain its sovereignty and independence in the face of global challenges and pressures.

The Foundations of Canada's Political System
Canada's political system is rooted in the British parliamentary tradition, which emphasizes the fusion of executive and legislative powers. At the heart of this system is the principle of responsible government, which holds that the executive branch (the Prime Minister and Cabinet) must maintain the confidence of the elected legislature (the House of Commons). This principle ensures that the government is accountable to the people through their elected representatives.

The British North America Act (BNA Act) of 1867, which established Canada as a federation, laid the groundwork for the country's political system. The BNA Act divided powers between the federal and provincial governments, creating a balance between central authority and regional autonomy. This federal structure has allowed Canada to accommodate its vast geographic and cultural diversity, while maintaining a unified national government.

The Role of the Monarchy

Canada's status as a constitutional monarchy is another defining feature of its political system. The British monarch, currently King Charles III, serves as Canada's head of state, represented domestically by the Governor General. While the role of the monarchy is largely ceremonial, it serves as a symbol of continuity and tradition, linking Canada to its historical ties with the British Empire.

The monarchy also plays a unifying role in Canada's federal system. As the head of state, the monarch represents all Canadians, regardless of their province or territory. This symbolic role helps to balance the diverse regional and cultural interests within Canada, reinforcing the nation's commitment to unity and inclusivity.

The Parliamentary System

Canada's parliamentary system is characterized by the fusion of executive and legislative powers. The Prime Minister, who is the head of government, is typically the leader of the political party that holds the most seats in the House of Commons. The Prime Minister and Cabinet are drawn from the elected members of Parliament, ensuring that the executive branch is directly accountable to the legislature.

This system contrasts sharply with the U.S. presidential system, where the executive branch is separate from the legislature and the President is elected independently. The parliamentary system allows for greater flexibility and responsiveness, as the government can be replaced without the need for a fixed-term election if it loses the confidence of the legislature.

Federalism and Regional Autonomy

Canada's federal structure is a key component of its political system, allowing for the accommodation of regional and cultural differences. The division of powers between the federal and provincial governments is outlined in the Constitution Act, 1867, with the federal government responsible for areas such as defense, foreign policy, and trade, and the provinces responsible for areas such as education, healthcare, and natural resources.

This division of powers has enabled Canada to balance the need for a strong central government with the desire for regional autonomy. It has also allowed provinces like Quebec to preserve their distinct cultural and linguistic identity, while remaining part of the broader Canadian federation.

The Charter of Rights and Freedoms

The Canadian Charter of Rights and Freedoms, enacted as part of the Constitution Act, 1982, is a cornerstone of Canada's political system. The Charter guarantees fundamental rights and freedoms to all Canadians, including freedom of expression, freedom of religion, and equality before the law. It also includes provisions to protect minority language rights, reflecting Canada's commitment to bilingualism and multiculturalism.

The Charter has had a profound impact on Canadian society, shaping the country's approach to issues such as civil liberties, social justice, and human rights. It has also served as a powerful tool for individuals and groups seeking to challenge discriminatory laws and practices, reinforcing Canada's reputation as a just and inclusive society.

The Role of the Judiciary

Canada's judiciary plays a crucial role in upholding the rule of law and interpreting the Constitution. The Supreme Court of Canada, established in 1875, is the highest court in the country and serves as the final arbiter of legal disputes. The Court's decisions have had a significant impact on Canadian society, particularly in areas such as Indigenous rights, gender equality, and civil liberties.

The independence of the judiciary is a key feature of Canada's political system, ensuring that the courts are free from political interference and can act as a check on the power of the executive and legislative branches. This independence is essential for maintaining the rule of law and protecting the rights and freedoms of Canadians.

Challenges to Political Sovereignty

Despite its strengths, Canada's political system faces ongoing challenges to its sovereignty and independence. The country's close economic and political ties to the United States have raised concerns about the potential for undue influence and interference. For example, provisions in trade agreements such as NAFTA and the USMCA have been criticized for limiting Canada's ability to regulate industries and protect its cultural identity.

Canada's commitment to multilateralism and global governance also presents challenges, as it requires the country to navigate complex international relationships and balance competing interests. The rise of populism and nationalism in other parts of the world has further complicated this landscape, creating new pressures and uncertainties for Canadian policymakers.

The Future of Canadian Governance
As Canada continues to evolve, so too will its political system and governance structure. The country's ability to maintain its sovereignty and independence will depend on its ability to adapt to changing circumstances and address emerging challenges. This will require a renewed commitment to the principles of democracy, accountability, and inclusivity, as well as a willingness to engage with the global community in a spirit of cooperation and mutual respect.

Conclusion: A Model of Sovereignty and Governance
Canada's political system and governance structure are a testament to the country's ability to balance tradition and innovation, unity and diversity, and independence and interdependence. By understanding the key features of this system, we can better appreciate the forces that have shaped Canada's development and ensured its continued success.

In a world that is increasingly interconnected and complex, Canada's political system offers a model for how nations can navigate the challenges of governance and sovereignty. It is a model that reflects the values of democracy, accountability, and inclusivity—values that are at the heart of what it means to be Canadian. By upholding these values, Canada can continue to thrive as a sovereign and independent nation, while contributing to the global community in meaningful and impactful ways.

Chapter 9: Defense and Security

Canada's approach to defense and security is a critical component of its sovereignty and independence. As a nation with a vast territory, a relatively small population, and a long border with the United States, Canada faces unique challenges in ensuring its security while maintaining its commitment to peacekeeping, multilateralism, and international cooperation. This chapter explores Canada's defense and security strategies, highlighting how the country has balanced its relationship with the United States, its role in global peacekeeping, and its efforts to protect its sovereignty in an increasingly complex and interconnected world.

The Foundations of Canadian Defense Policy

Canada's defense policy has historically been shaped by its geographic location, its relationship with the British Empire, and its commitment to international peace and security. During the colonial period, Canada relied on British military protection, particularly in the face of threats from the United States, such as during the War of 1812. However, as Canada evolved into a self-governing dominion and later a fully sovereign nation, it began to develop its own defense capabilities and policies.

The two World Wars marked a turning point in Canada's defense policy, as the country made significant contributions to the Allied war efforts. These contributions not only demonstrated Canada's military capabilities but also reinforced its commitment to international peace and security. In the post-war period, Canada emerged as a leading advocate for multilateralism and collective security, playing a key role in the establishment of the United Nations and NATO.

The Role of NATO and Collective Security

Canada's membership in NATO has been a cornerstone of its defense policy since the alliance's founding in 1949. As a founding member, Canada has played an active role in NATO's missions and operations, contributing troops, resources, and expertise to collective defense efforts. NATO membership has provided Canada with a framework for cooperation with other democratic nations, enhancing its security and reinforcing its commitment to international peace and stability.

Canada's contributions to NATO have also served as a counterbalance to its close relationship with the United States. While the U.S. is Canada's most important ally and trading partner, NATO membership allows Canada to maintain a degree of independence and flexibility in its defense policy. This has been particularly important in situations where Canadian and U.S. interests diverge, such as during the Vietnam War and the Iraq War.

Peacekeeping and Multilateralism

Canada's commitment to peacekeeping is one of the most distinctive aspects of its defense policy. Since the mid-20th century, Canada has been a leading contributor to UN peacekeeping missions, earning a reputation as a neutral and impartial mediator. The image of Canadian peacekeepers as protectors of vulnerable populations and promoters of peace has become a source of national pride and a key element of Canada's international identity.

Canada's peacekeeping efforts have also reinforced its commitment to multilateralism and international cooperation. By participating in UN missions, Canada has demonstrated its belief in the importance of collective action and the rule of law in addressing global security challenges. This commitment to multilateralism sets Canada apart from more unilateral approaches to defense and security, such as those often pursued by the United States.

The Canada-U.S. Defense Relationship
Canada's defense relationship with the United States is one of the most important and complex aspects of its security policy. The two nations share the longest undefended border in the world and have a long history of military cooperation, particularly in the context of NATO and NORAD (the North American Aerospace Defense Command).

NORAD, established in 1958, is a binational command responsible for aerospace warning and control, as well as maritime warning. It represents a unique example of military cooperation between two sovereign nations, reflecting the deep trust and interdependence between Canada and the United States. However, this relationship also presents challenges, as Canada must balance its close ties to the U.S. with the need to maintain its independence and sovereignty.

Challenges to Canadian Security

Canada faces a range of security challenges in the 21st century, including cyber threats, terrorism, climate change, and the resurgence of great power competition. These challenges require a comprehensive and adaptive approach to defense and security, as well as a commitment to international cooperation and innovation.

Cyber security, in particular, has emerged as a critical issue for Canada, as the country's reliance on digital infrastructure makes it vulnerable to cyber attacks. The Canadian government has taken steps to enhance its cyber defenses, including the establishment of the Canadian Centre for Cyber Security and the development of a national cyber security strategy.

Climate change also poses significant security challenges for Canada, particularly in the Arctic. As the region becomes more accessible due to melting ice, Canada must contend with increased military activity, resource competition, and environmental risks. The Canadian government has responded by investing in Arctic defense capabilities, such as new icebreakers and surveillance systems, and by working with international partners to promote sustainable development in the region.

The Future of Canadian Defense and Security

As Canada looks to the future, its defense and security policies will need to adapt to emerging challenges and opportunities. This will require a renewed commitment to innovation, collaboration, and strategic thinking, as well as a willingness to invest in new technologies and capabilities.

Canada's commitment to peacekeeping and multilateralism will remain a key element of its defense policy, reflecting the country's values and priorities. At the same time, Canada will need to strengthen its domestic security capabilities, particularly in areas such as cyber security and Arctic defense, to address emerging threats and protect its sovereignty.

Conclusion: A Balanced Approach to Defense and Security
Canada's approach to defense and security reflects its unique position as a middle power with a commitment to peacekeeping, multilateralism, and international cooperation. By balancing its close relationship with the United States with its commitment to global peace and security, Canada has been able to maintain its sovereignty and independence while contributing to the stability and security of the international community.

In a world that is increasingly interconnected and complex, Canada's defense and security policies offer a model for how nations can navigate the challenges of the 21st century. It is a model that reflects the values of peace, cooperation, and resilience—values that are at the heart of what it means to be Canadian. By upholding these values, Canada can continue to thrive as a sovereign and independent nation, while contributing to the global community in meaningful and impactful ways.

Chapter 10: The Legacy of the British Empire

Canada's relationship with the British Empire has left an indelible mark on its national identity, political institutions, and cultural heritage. From its origins as a collection of British colonies to its evolution into a fully sovereign nation, Canada's ties to the British Empire have shaped its development in profound and lasting ways. This chapter explores the legacy of the British Empire in Canada, examining how it has influenced the country's governance, culture, and identity, and why it continues to play a role in Canada's distinctiveness as a nation.

The Colonial Foundations of Canada
Canada's history as part of the British Empire begins with the colonization of North America by European powers. Following the defeat of France in the Seven Years' War (1756–1763), Britain gained control of most of France's North American territories, including what is now Quebec. The Royal Proclamation of 1763 and the Quebec Act of 1774 were early attempts by Britain to manage its new colonies, balancing the interests of French-speaking Catholics with those of English-speaking Protestants.

The arrival of United Empire Loyalists after the American Revolution further solidified British influence in Canada. These Loyalists, who remained loyal to the British Crown, brought with them a commitment to British institutions and values, which became deeply embedded in Canadian society. This early period of colonization laid the groundwork for Canada's development as a British colony and, eventually, a self-governing dominion.

The Evolution of Self-Governance

Canada's path to self-governance within the British Empire was marked by gradual evolution rather than revolutionary change. The Constitutional Act of 1791 established representative governments in Upper and Lower Canada, while the Act of Union of 1841 united the two colonies into the Province of Canada. These steps toward self-governance culminated in Confederation in 1867, when the British North America Act created the Dominion of Canada.

Confederation granted Canada a significant degree of autonomy, particularly in domestic affairs, while maintaining ties to the British Empire. The new federal system of government allowed Canada to balance regional and cultural differences, setting the stage for its development as a unified and independent nation.

The Role of the Monarchy

The British monarchy has played a central role in Canada's political and cultural identity. As a constitutional monarchy, Canada recognizes the British monarch as its head of state, represented domestically by the Governor General. While the role of the monarchy is largely ceremonial, it serves as a symbol of continuity and tradition, linking Canada to its historical ties with the British Empire.

The monarchy also plays a unifying role in Canada's federal system. As the head of state, the monarch represents all Canadians, regardless of their province or territory. This symbolic role helps to balance the diverse regional and cultural interests within Canada, reinforcing the nation's commitment to unity and inclusivity.

The Statute of Westminster and Legislative Independence

Canada's journey to full sovereignty reached a critical milestone with the Statute of Westminster of 1931. This legislation, passed by the British Parliament, granted Canada and other dominions (such as Australia and New Zealand) full legislative independence. No longer was Canada subject to British laws or oversight; it was free to make its own decisions in all areas, including foreign policy and defense.

The Statute of Westminster was a recognition of Canada's growing maturity as a nation. By the early 20th century, Canada had proven its ability to govern itself, both domestically and internationally. Its contributions to World War I, particularly at battles such as Vimy Ridge, had demonstrated its commitment to the Empire while also asserting its distinct identity. The Statute of Westminster formalized this reality, marking Canada's transition from a dominion to a fully sovereign nation.

The Commonwealth of Nations

Canada's ties to the British Empire have evolved into a modern relationship with the Commonwealth of Nations. The Commonwealth, a voluntary association of countries with historical links to Britain, provides Canada with a platform to engage with other nations on issues of mutual concern, from trade to climate change. While the Commonwealth no longer holds the same political significance as the British Empire, it remains an important symbol of Canada's historical and cultural connections to Britain and the wider world.

Canada's active role in the Commonwealth reflects its commitment to multilateralism and international cooperation. By participating in Commonwealth initiatives, Canada has been able to promote its values and interests on the global stage, while maintaining its ties to its historical roots.

The Legacy of British Institutions

The legacy of the British Empire is evident in Canada's political and legal institutions. Canada's parliamentary system, based on the British model, emphasizes the fusion of executive and legislative powers and the principle of responsible government. This system has provided Canada with a stable and adaptable framework for governance, allowing it to navigate the challenges of a diverse and rapidly changing society.

Canada's legal system, rooted in English common law, also reflects its British heritage. The principles of the rule of law, judicial independence, and the protection of individual rights are central to Canada's legal framework, as enshrined in the Canadian Charter of Rights and Freedoms. These principles have shaped Canada's approach to justice and human rights, reinforcing its reputation as a just and inclusive society.

Cultural and Social Influences

The influence of the British Empire extends beyond Canada's political and legal institutions to its culture and society. British traditions, such as the celebration of the monarch's birthday and the use of British symbols (e.g., the Union Jack in some provincial flags), are still evident in Canadian life. The English language, which is one of Canada's two official languages, is another legacy of British colonization.

At the same time, Canada's multicultural identity has evolved to incorporate the contributions of people from around the world, creating a society that is both rooted in British traditions and open to diverse influences. This blending of old and new, tradition and innovation, is a defining feature of Canadian culture.

Challenges and Criticisms

While the legacy of the British Empire has shaped Canada in many positive ways, it is not without its challenges and criticisms. The history of colonization has had lasting impacts on Indigenous peoples, who continue to face systemic inequalities and the legacy of residential schools. The process of reconciliation, as outlined in the Truth and Reconciliation Commission (2015), is an ongoing effort to address these injustices and build a more inclusive and equitable society.

Similarly, Canada's ties to the British monarchy have been the subject of debate, particularly as the country continues to evolve as a multicultural and independent nation. Some argue that the monarchy is an outdated institution that no longer reflects Canada's diverse and modern identity, while others see it as a valuable link to the country's history and traditions.

Conclusion: A Living Legacy

The legacy of the British Empire is a living and evolving part of Canada's identity. It has shaped the country's political institutions, cultural heritage, and national character, providing a foundation for its development as a sovereign and independent nation. At the same time, Canada's ability to adapt and innovate within this framework has allowed it to embrace diversity and change, creating a society that is both rooted in tradition and open to the future.

By understanding the legacy of the British Empire, we can better appreciate the forces that have shaped Canada's past and continue to guide its future. It is a legacy that reflects the values of stability, continuity, and resilience—values that are at the heart of what it means to be Canadian. In a world that is increasingly interconnected and complex, Canada's ability to balance tradition and innovation serves as a model for how nations can navigate the challenges of the 21st century while remaining true to their heritage.

Chapter 11: The Commonwealth Connection

Canada's membership in the Commonwealth of Nations is a testament to its historical ties to the British Empire and its commitment to international cooperation and multilateralism. As one of the founding members of the Commonwealth, Canada has played a significant role in shaping the organization's mission and values, while also benefiting from its opportunities for collaboration and dialogue. This chapter explores Canada's relationship with the Commonwealth, highlighting its contributions to the organization, the benefits of membership, and how this connection reinforces Canada's distinct identity and global presence.

The Origins of the Commonwealth

The Commonwealth of Nations traces its origins to the gradual decolonization of the British Empire in the 20th century. As former colonies gained independence, they sought to maintain their ties to Britain and to each other through a voluntary association based on shared values and interests. The modern Commonwealth was formally established with the London Declaration of 1949, which recognized member states as "free and equal" and allowed republics to remain part of the organization while acknowledging the British monarch as the symbolic head of the Commonwealth.

Canada, as one of the original dominions of the British Empire, was a founding member of the Commonwealth. Its participation in the organization reflects its historical ties to Britain and its commitment to fostering cooperation and understanding among nations with diverse cultures, histories, and political systems.

Canada's Role in the Commonwealth

Canada has been an active and influential member of the Commonwealth since its inception. The country has played a key role in shaping the organization's mission and priorities, particularly in areas such as democracy, human rights, and sustainable development. Canada's contributions to the Commonwealth have included financial support, technical expertise, and leadership in various initiatives and programs.

One of Canada's most significant contributions to the Commonwealth has been its advocacy for inclusive and equitable development. Through initiatives such as the Commonwealth Fund for Technical Cooperation (CFTC), Canada has supported capacity-building and knowledge-sharing among member states, particularly in developing countries. Canada has also been a strong proponent of gender equality and women's empowerment within the Commonwealth, championing initiatives to promote women's leadership and economic participation.

The Benefits of Commonwealth Membership

Membership in the Commonwealth offers Canada a range of benefits, both tangible and symbolic. On a practical level, the Commonwealth provides Canada with a platform for diplomatic engagement and collaboration on issues of mutual concern, such as trade, climate change, and public health. The organization's diverse membership, which includes countries from Africa, Asia, the Caribbean, and the Pacific, allows Canada to build relationships and partnerships with nations that it might not otherwise engage with on a regular basis.

The Commonwealth also offers opportunities for cultural exchange and people-to-people connections. Programs such as the Commonwealth Scholarship and Fellowship Plan enable students and professionals from member states to study and work in Canada, fostering mutual understanding and collaboration. Similarly, events such as the Commonwealth Games provide a platform for cultural and sporting exchange, strengthening the bonds between member states.

On a symbolic level, Canada's membership in the Commonwealth reinforces its historical ties to Britain and its identity as a nation with a global perspective. The Commonwealth's emphasis on shared values such as democracy, human rights, and the rule of law aligns with Canada's own values and priorities, providing a framework for its engagement with the international community.

The Commonwealth and Canada's Global Identity

Canada's participation in the Commonwealth is an important aspect of its global identity. As a middle power with a commitment to multilateralism and international cooperation, Canada has used its membership in the Commonwealth to promote its values and interests on the global stage. The organization's emphasis on consensus-building and dialogue aligns with Canada's approach to diplomacy, allowing it to play a constructive and influential role in addressing global challenges.

The Commonwealth also provides Canada with a unique platform for engaging with small states and developing countries, which make up the majority of the organization's membership. By supporting initiatives that promote sustainable development, good governance, and social inclusion, Canada has been able to contribute to the well-being of some of the world's most vulnerable populations, while also advancing its own interests in a stable and prosperous global community.

Challenges and Opportunities
While the Commonwealth offers many benefits, it also faces challenges that reflect the complexities of the modern world. The organization's diverse membership includes countries with varying levels of economic development, political systems, and cultural traditions, which can make it difficult to achieve consensus on key issues. Additionally, the Commonwealth's reliance on voluntary contributions and its limited institutional capacity have sometimes constrained its ability to implement programs and initiatives effectively.

For Canada, these challenges present both risks and opportunities. On the one hand, Canada must navigate the complexities of engaging with a diverse and sometimes divided membership. On the other hand, the Commonwealth's emphasis on dialogue and cooperation provides Canada with opportunities to demonstrate leadership and build bridges between different regions and cultures.

The Future of Canada's Commonwealth Connection

As the Commonwealth continues to evolve, Canada's role within the organization will likely adapt to reflect changing global realities. The rise of new economic powers, the growing importance of climate change and sustainability, and the increasing interconnectedness of the global community will all shape the Commonwealth's priorities and Canada's contributions to the organization.

Canada's commitment to the Commonwealth's values and principles will remain a key aspect of its foreign policy. By continuing to support initiatives that promote democracy, human rights, and sustainable development, Canada can help to ensure that the Commonwealth remains a relevant and effective force for good in the world.

Conclusion: A Bridge to the World

Canada's connection to the Commonwealth is a reflection of its historical ties to the British Empire and its commitment to international cooperation and multilateralism. Through its participation in the Commonwealth, Canada has been able to build relationships, promote its values, and contribute to the well-being of people around the world.

The Commonwealth provides Canada with a unique platform for engaging with a diverse and dynamic group of nations, fostering dialogue and collaboration on issues of mutual concern. In a world that is increasingly interconnected and complex, Canada's Commonwealth connection serves as a bridge to the global community, reinforcing its identity as a nation that is both rooted in tradition and open to the future.

By understanding the significance of the Commonwealth, we can better appreciate the forces that have shaped Canada's global presence and its commitment to building a more just, inclusive, and sustainable world. It is a commitment that reflects the values of cooperation, dialogue, and mutual respect—values that are at the heart of what it means to be Canadian.

Chapter 12: Canada on the World Stage

Canada's role on the global stage is defined by its commitment to multilateralism, peacekeeping, and international cooperation. As a middle power with a strong tradition of diplomacy and a reputation for fairness, Canada has consistently punched above its weight in international affairs. This chapter explores Canada's contributions to global peace and security, its leadership in addressing global challenges, and how its actions on the world stage reinforce its sovereignty and distinct identity. From its role in founding the United Nations to its advocacy for climate action and human rights, Canada's global presence reflects its values and priorities as a nation.

A Tradition of Multilateralism

Canada's commitment to multilateralism is one of the defining features of its foreign policy. Unlike larger powers that may pursue unilateral or hegemonic strategies, Canada has consistently sought to work within international institutions and frameworks to address global challenges. This approach is rooted in the belief that collective action and cooperation are essential for achieving peace, security, and prosperity.

Canada's role in the founding of the United Nations (UN) in 1945 is a prime example of its commitment to multilateralism. As one of the original signatories of the UN Charter, Canada played a key role in shaping the organization's mission and principles. Since then, Canada has been an active participant in UN initiatives, from peacekeeping missions to humanitarian aid programs, earning a reputation as a reliable and constructive partner.

Peacekeeping: A Canadian Legacy

Canada's contributions to international peacekeeping are among its most celebrated achievements on the world stage. The concept of peacekeeping was pioneered by Canadian diplomat and future Prime Minister Lester B. Pearson, who proposed the idea during the Suez Crisis of 1956. For his efforts, Pearson was awarded the Nobel Peace Prize, and Canada became synonymous with peacekeeping.

Over the decades, Canadian peacekeepers have served in some of the world's most challenging conflict zones, from Cyprus to the Balkans, from Rwanda to Haiti. While Canada's contributions to peacekeeping have diminished in recent years due to shifting priorities and budget constraints, the legacy of Canadian peacekeeping remains a source of national pride and a key element of the country's international identity.

Human Rights and Humanitarian Leadership

Canada has long been a champion of human rights and humanitarian causes on the global stage. From its advocacy for the Universal Declaration of Human Rights to its leadership in the fight against apartheid in South Africa, Canada has consistently used its voice and influence to promote justice and equality.

One of Canada's most notable contributions to human rights was its role in the establishment of the International Criminal Court (ICC). Canadian diplomat Philippe Kirsch played a key role in drafting the Rome Statute, the treaty that created the ICC, and served as the court's first president. Canada's support for the ICC reflects its commitment to accountability and the rule of law in addressing international crimes such as genocide, war crimes, and crimes against humanity.

Canada has also been a leader in humanitarian aid and disaster relief. Through organizations such as the Canadian Red Cross and Global Affairs Canada, the country has provided assistance to communities affected by natural disasters, conflicts, and health crises. Canada's response to the Syrian refugee crisis, which included the resettlement of tens of thousands of refugees, is a recent example of its humanitarian leadership.

Climate Action and Sustainable Development
As the global community faces the urgent challenge of climate change, Canada has emerged as a leader in promoting sustainable development and environmental protection. The country played a key role in the negotiation of the Paris Agreement, a landmark international treaty aimed at limiting global warming to well below 2 degrees Celsius. Canada has also committed to ambitious domestic climate targets, including achieving net-zero emissions by 2050.

Canada's leadership in sustainable development extends beyond climate action. The country has been a strong advocate for the United Nations' Sustainable Development Goals (SDGs), which provide a framework for addressing global challenges such as poverty, inequality, and environmental degradation. Through initiatives such as the Feminist International Assistance Policy, Canada has integrated gender equality and social inclusion into its development efforts, ensuring that the benefits of progress are shared by all.

Diplomatic Leadership and Conflict Resolution

Canada's reputation as a fair and impartial mediator has made it a sought-after partner in diplomatic efforts to resolve conflicts and promote peace. The country's role in the Camp David Accords, which led to a peace treaty between Israel and Egypt, is a notable example of its diplomatic leadership. More recently, Canada has been involved in efforts to address conflicts in regions such as Ukraine, Myanmar, and Venezuela, using its diplomatic channels to advocate for dialogue and peaceful solutions.

Canada's diplomatic efforts are guided by its commitment to inclusivity and respect for diversity. The country's multicultural identity and bilingualism provide it with unique insights and connections that enhance its ability to engage with a wide range of actors on the global stage.

Challenges and Criticisms

Despite its many achievements, Canada's role on the world stage is not without its challenges and criticisms. The country's reliance on natural resource exports, particularly oil and gas, has sometimes put it at odds with its climate commitments, leading to criticism from environmental advocates. Similarly, Canada's arms exports to countries with questionable human rights records have raised concerns about the consistency of its foreign policy.

Canada's diminished contributions to UN peacekeeping in recent years have also been a source of criticism. While the country continues to support peacekeeping in principle, its actual deployments have declined, leading some to question its commitment to this legacy.

The Future of Canada's Global Role
As the world becomes increasingly interconnected and complex, Canada's role on the global stage will continue to evolve. The rise of new economic powers, the growing threat of climate change, and the resurgence of geopolitical tensions present both challenges and opportunities for Canadian diplomacy.

To maintain its influence and relevance, Canada will need to adapt its foreign policy to reflect changing global realities. This will require a renewed commitment to multilateralism, increased investment in diplomacy and development, and a willingness to address emerging issues such as cyber security, artificial intelligence, and global health.

Conclusion: A Voice for Peace and Progress
Canada's role on the world stage is a reflection of its values and priorities as a nation. From its contributions to peacekeeping and human rights to its leadership in climate action and sustainable development, Canada has consistently demonstrated its commitment to building a more just, inclusive, and sustainable world.

By understanding Canada's global contributions, we can better appreciate the forces that have shaped its identity and ensured its continued success. In a world that is increasingly divided and uncertain, Canada's voice for peace and progress serves as a reminder of the importance of cooperation, dialogue, and mutual respect. It is a voice that reflects the values of fairness, compassion, and resilience—values that are at the heart of what it means to be Canadian.

Chapter 13: The Myth of Annexation

The idea of Canada becoming the 51st state of the United States is a notion that has persisted for decades, often surfacing in casual conversations, political debates, and even popular culture. While the two nations share a long border, deep economic ties, and cultural similarities, the idea of annexation is fundamentally at odds with Canada's history, identity, and aspirations. This chapter explores the origins of the annexation myth, debunks the arguments in favor of it, and explains why Canada will never become part of the United States.

The Origins of the Annexation Myth

The idea of Canada joining the United States is not new. It dates back to the American Revolution, when some American leaders envisioned a continent united under one flag. The War of 1812, during which the U.S. attempted to invade British North America, was partly motivated by the desire to annex Canadian territory. Although the invasion failed, the idea of annexation persisted, particularly among American expansionists who embraced the ideology of Manifest Destiny—the belief that the U.S. was destined to expand across the continent.

In the 19th century, there were sporadic movements in Canada advocating for annexation, particularly among business elites who saw economic benefits in closer ties with the U.S. However, these movements never gained widespread support, as most Canadians valued their ties to Britain and their distinct identity. The idea of annexation resurfaced during times of economic or political uncertainty, but it was always met with strong resistance from the Canadian public and political leaders.

Debunking the Arguments for Annexation

Proponents of annexation often argue that Canada would benefit from joining the United States, citing economic, political, and cultural reasons. However, these arguments fail to account for the profound differences between the two nations and the values that define Canadian identity.

1. Economic Integration vs. Sovereignty: While Canada and the U.S. share a deeply integrated economy, this does not equate to a desire for political union. Canadians take pride in their economic independence and their ability to negotiate trade agreements on their own terms. Joining the U.S. would mean surrendering control over key economic policies, such as healthcare, taxation, and natural resource management.

2. Political and Cultural Differences: Canada's political system, based on parliamentary democracy and constitutional monarchy, is fundamentally different from the U.S. presidential system. Canadians value their traditions of inclusivity, moderation, and social welfare, which are often at odds with American individualism and free-market ideology. The cultural differences between the two nations, particularly Canada's commitment to bilingualism and multiculturalism, further underscore the challenges of annexation.

3. Quebec's Resistance: Quebec's distinct cultural and linguistic identity makes the idea of annexation particularly untenable. Quebecers have long

fought to preserve their language and culture within Canada, and the prospect of joining the U.S. would be met with fierce opposition. Quebec's presence in the Canadian federation is a key reason why annexation is not a viable option.

4.Public Opinion: Polls consistently show that the vast majority of Canadians oppose the idea of joining the United States. Canadians take pride in their country's independence, its global reputation, and its distinct identity. The idea of becoming the 51st state is seen as a betrayal of these values and a loss of national sovereignty.

The Logistical Challenges of Annexation
Even if there were a desire for annexation, the logistical challenges would be insurmountable. Canada and the U.S. have vastly different political, legal, and administrative systems, which would need to be reconciled in the event of a merger. Issues such as healthcare, education, taxation, and natural resource management would require complex negotiations and compromises, likely leading to significant disruptions and dissatisfaction on both sides.

Moreover, the process of annexation would require the consent of both nations, as well as constitutional amendments in both countries. Given the strong opposition to annexation in Canada and the lack of interest in the U.S., the likelihood of such an agreement being reached is virtually nonexistent.

Canada's Commitment to Sovereignty

Canada's history is one of gradual evolution toward full sovereignty, marked by a commitment to peaceful change and self-determination. From Confederation in 1867 to the Statute of Westminster in 1931 and the patriation of the Constitution in 1982, Canada has carefully navigated its path to independence while maintaining its ties to the British Crown and the Commonwealth.

This commitment to sovereignty is deeply ingrained in the Canadian psyche. Canadians take pride in their ability to govern themselves, to make their own decisions, and to chart their own course in the world. The idea of surrendering this sovereignty to join the United States is antithetical to everything Canada stands for.

The Symbolic Importance of Independence

Canada's independence is not just a matter of practical governance; it is also a source of national pride and identity. Canadians value their country's reputation as a peacekeeper, a mediator, and a champion of human rights. They take pride in their multicultural society, their universal healthcare system, and their commitment to social welfare. These achievements are a reflection of Canada's distinct values and priorities, which would be fundamentally altered by annexation.

The idea of becoming the 51st state is seen as a loss of identity, a betrayal of Canada's history, and a rejection of its aspirations for the future. It is an idea that resonates with few Canadians and is firmly rooted in myth rather than reality.

Conclusion: A Sovereign Future

The myth of annexation is a reflection of the deep ties between Canada and the United States, but it is also a reminder of the profound differences that define the two nations. Canada's commitment to sovereignty, its distinct identity, and its values of inclusivity, moderation, and social welfare make the idea of joining the U.S. both impractical and undesirable.

By understanding the origins and implications of the annexation myth, we can better appreciate the forces that have shaped Canada's development and ensured its continued independence. Canada's story is one of resilience, adaptability, and quiet determination—a story that reflects the values of peace, cooperation, and self-determination. In a world that is increasingly interconnected and complex, Canada's sovereignty serves as a reminder of the importance of preserving national identity and charting one's own course. It is a reminder that Canada's future lies not in becoming the 51st state, but in continuing to thrive as a sovereign and independent nation.

The Myth of Canada Becoming the 51st State

Chapter 14: Strengthening Canadian Identity in the 21st Century

As Canada moves further into the 21st century, the task of strengthening and preserving its national identity becomes increasingly important. In a world marked by globalization, technological advancements, and shifting geopolitical dynamics, Canada faces both opportunities and challenges in defining what it means to be Canadian. This chapter explores the strategies and initiatives that can help reinforce Canadian identity, ensuring that it remains vibrant, inclusive, and resilient in the face of change. From education and media to cultural institutions and public policy, Canada must leverage its strengths and address its weaknesses to build a cohesive and dynamic national identity.

The Role of Education

Education is one of the most powerful tools for shaping and reinforcing national identity. By teaching students about Canada's history, values, and cultural diversity, schools can foster a sense of pride and belonging among young Canadians. This includes not only the study of key historical events, such as Confederation and the contributions of Indigenous peoples, but also an understanding of Canada's role in global affairs, from peacekeeping to climate action.

Efforts to incorporate Indigenous perspectives and histories into the curriculum are particularly important. The Truth and Reconciliation Commission (2015) called for education to play a central role in reconciliation, emphasizing the need to teach students about the legacy of residential schools and the ongoing impacts of colonialism. By doing so, Canada can build a more inclusive and accurate understanding of its history and identity.

The Power of Media and Storytelling
Media and storytelling play a crucial role in shaping how Canadians see themselves and their country. Canadian films, television shows, literature, and music provide a platform for sharing diverse voices and experiences, reflecting the richness of Canada's cultural mosaic. Supporting Canadian content through initiatives such as the Canadian Media Fund and the Canada Council for the Arts ensures that these stories continue to be told and celebrated.

At the same time, Canada must address the challenges posed by digital media and globalization. The dominance of American and international content on digital platforms can overshadow Canadian voices, making it harder for homegrown stories to reach audiences. By investing in digital innovation and promoting Canadian content online, Canada can ensure that its cultural identity remains strong in the digital age.

Cultural Institutions and Public Spaces
Cultural institutions, such as museums, galleries, and libraries, are vital for preserving and promoting Canadian identity. These institutions provide spaces for Canadians to explore their history, celebrate their achievements, and engage with diverse perspectives. Initiatives such as the Canadian Museum for Human Rights and the National Gallery of

Canada showcase the country's commitment to inclusivity, creativity, and social justice.

Public spaces, such as parks, monuments, and community centers, also play a role in fostering a sense of belonging and shared identity. Events such as Canada Day celebrations, multicultural festivals, and Indigenous cultural gatherings bring Canadians together, reinforcing the values of unity and diversity.

The Importance of Bilingualism and Multiculturalism
Canada's commitment to bilingualism and multiculturalism is a defining feature of its national identity. The Official Languages Act and the Canadian Multiculturalism Act provide a legal framework for protecting and promoting linguistic and cultural diversity. These policies reflect Canada's belief that diversity is a strength, not a weakness, and that all Canadians should have the opportunity to contribute to the national fabric.

Efforts to support Indigenous languages and cultures are also essential. The Indigenous Languages Act (2019) is a step in the right direction, recognizing the importance of preserving and revitalizing Indigenous languages. By embracing its linguistic and cultural diversity, Canada can build a more inclusive and resilient national identity.

Public Policy and National Values
Public policy plays a key role in shaping and reinforcing national identity. Programs such as universal healthcare, affordable childcare, and social safety nets reflect Canada's commitment to equity, compassion, and the

common good. These policies are not just practical measures; they are expressions of Canadian values, reinforcing the idea that everyone deserves a fair chance to succeed.

At the same time, Canada must address the challenges of inequality, discrimination, and social exclusion. The Truth and Reconciliation Commission and the National Inquiry into Missing and Murdered Indigenous Women and Girls have highlighted the need for systemic change to address the legacy of colonialism and build a more just and inclusive society. By tackling these issues head-on, Canada can strengthen its identity as a nation that values fairness, justice, and human rights.

The Role of Global Leadership
Canada's role on the world stage is another important aspect of its national identity. By continuing to champion peacekeeping, multilateralism, and climate action, Canada can reinforce its reputation as a responsible and compassionate global citizen. This includes supporting international organizations such as the United Nations, participating in global initiatives to address climate change, and advocating for human rights and social justice.

Canada's global leadership also provides an opportunity to showcase its values and priorities to the world. By sharing its experiences with multiculturalism, bilingualism, and reconciliation, Canada can inspire other nations to embrace diversity and inclusivity.

Challenges and Opportunities in the 21st Century

The 21st century presents both challenges and opportunities for strengthening Canadian identity. Globalization, technological change, and shifting demographics are reshaping the world, creating new pressures and possibilities for Canada. The rise of populism and nationalism in other parts of the world underscores the importance of promoting inclusivity and dialogue, while the growing threat of climate change highlights the need for collective action and innovation.

Canada's ability to navigate these challenges will depend on its willingness to adapt and innovate. This includes investing in education, supporting cultural institutions, and addressing systemic inequalities. It also requires a commitment to dialogue and collaboration, both within Canada and on the global stage.

Conclusion: A Shared Vision for the Future

Strengthening Canadian identity in the 21st century is a shared responsibility that requires the efforts of all Canadians. By embracing its diversity, celebrating its achievements, and addressing its challenges, Canada can build a national identity that is vibrant, inclusive, and resilient.

This vision for the future reflects the values of peace, cooperation, and mutual respect—values that are at the heart of what it means to be Canadian. In a world that is increasingly interconnected and complex, Canada's ability to strengthen its identity will depend on its willingness to uphold these values and work together toward a common goal. It is a goal that reflects the best of Canada's past and the promise of its future—a future that is bright, inclusive, and full of possibility.

Chapter 15: Conclusion: A Sovereign Future

As we reflect on Canada's journey—its history, identity, and aspirations—it becomes clear that the nation's sovereignty and independence are not merely the result of historical circumstance, but the product of deliberate choices, shared values, and a collective commitment to self-determination. This concluding chapter synthesizes the key themes explored throughout the book, emphasizing why Canada will not become the 51st state of the United States and how its unique identity ensures a sovereign and vibrant future.

The Pillars of Canadian Sovereignty

Canada's sovereignty rests on several foundational pillars, each of which has been carefully cultivated over centuries:

1.Historical Evolution: Unlike the United States, which achieved independence through revolution, Canada's path to sovereignty was marked by gradual evolution within the framework of the British Empire. This process, from Confederation to the Statute of Westminster and the patriation of the Constitution, reflects Canada's preference for stability, continuity, and peaceful change.

2.Cultural and Linguistic Diversity: Canada's commitment to bilingualism and multiculturalism sets it apart from many other nations. The recognition of French and English as official languages, the celebration of Indigenous cultures, and the embrace of immigrants from around the world have created a society that values inclusivity and diversity. This mosaic of identities is a source of strength and resilience, reinforcing Canada's distinctiveness.

3. Political and Institutional Independence: Canada's parliamentary system, constitutional monarchy, and federal structure provide a stable and adaptable framework for governance. These institutions reflect the nation's commitment to democracy, accountability, and the rule of law, ensuring that Canada remains a sovereign and self-governing nation.

4. Global Engagement and Multilateralism: Canada's role on the world stage—as a peacekeeper, mediator, and advocate for human rights—underscores its commitment to global cooperation and shared responsibility. By engaging with international organizations such as the United Nations and the Commonwealth, Canada has demonstrated its ability to contribute to global stability while maintaining its independence.

Why Canada Will Not Become the 51st State

The idea of Canada joining the United States is a myth that fails to account for the profound differences between the two nations. These differences are rooted in history, culture, and values, and they ensure that Canada's future lies in maintaining its sovereignty rather than surrendering it. Key reasons include:

-Cultural Identity: Canada's multicultural and bilingual identity is fundamentally different from the American "melting pot." Canadians take pride in their diversity and their ability to coexist within a shared national framework.

-Political Values: Canada's commitment to social welfare, universal healthcare, and inclusivity contrasts with the more individualistic and market-driven values of the United States. These differences reflect distinct approaches to governance and society.

-Quebec's Distinctiveness: Quebec's unique cultural and linguistic identity makes the idea of annexation particularly untenable. Quebecers have long fought to preserve their heritage within Canada, and the prospect of joining the U.S. would be met with fierce resistance.

-Public Opinion: The vast majority of Canadians oppose the idea of becoming part of the United States. Canadians value their independence, their global reputation, and their distinct identity, and they see no compelling reason to surrender these for the sake of annexation.

The Challenges Ahead

While Canada's sovereignty is secure, the nation faces significant challenges in the 21st century. These include:

-Reconciliation with Indigenous Peoples: Addressing the legacy of colonialism and building a more inclusive and equitable society is essential for Canada's future. The Truth and Reconciliation Commission and the National Inquiry into Missing and Murdered Indigenous Women and Girls have highlighted the need for systemic change and meaningful action.

-Climate Change and Sustainability: As a northern nation with vast natural resources, Canada is uniquely affected by climate change. The country must balance its economic interests with its commitment to environmental protection, ensuring a sustainable future for generations to come.

-Global Uncertainty: The rise of populism, nationalism, and geopolitical tensions presents challenges for Canada's global engagement. The nation must navigate these complexities while upholding its values and maintaining its independence.

A Vision for the Future
Canada's future lies in building on its strengths and addressing its challenges. This includes:

-Strengthening National Identity: By investing in education, supporting cultural institutions, and promoting Canadian content, Canada can reinforce its identity as a diverse, inclusive, and resilient nation.

-Championing Global Leadership: Canada's commitment to peacekeeping, multilateralism, and climate action positions it as a responsible and compassionate global citizen. By continuing to lead on these issues, Canada can contribute to a more just and sustainable world.

-Fostering Innovation and Adaptability: In a rapidly changing world, Canada must embrace innovation and adaptability. This includes investing in technology, supporting sustainable industries, and addressing systemic inequalities.

Conclusion: A Sovereign and Vibrant Future

Canada's sovereignty is not just a matter of political independence; it is a reflection of the nation's values, identity, and aspirations. By understanding the forces that have shaped Canada's past and present, we can better appreciate the importance of preserving its sovereignty and ensuring its continued success.

In a world that is increasingly interconnected and complex, Canada's ability to balance tradition and innovation, unity and diversity, and independence and interdependence serves as a model for other nations. It is a model that reflects the values of peace, cooperation, and mutual respect—values that are at the heart of what it means to be Canadian.

As Canada moves forward, it must remain true to these values, embracing the challenges and opportunities of the 21st century with resilience and determination. By doing so, Canada can continue to thrive as a sovereign and independent nation, contributing to the global community in meaningful and impactful ways. The story of Canada is one of quiet strength, adaptability, and hope—a story that inspires and endures, ensuring a bright and sovereign future for generations to come.

Appendices

The appendices provide supplementary information to enhance the reader's understanding of the themes and topics explored in the book. They include a timeline of key events in Canadian history, comparative data on Canada and the United States, and selected quotes from Canadian leaders on independence and sovereignty. These resources offer additional context and insights, helping to reinforce the book's central argument: that Canada's unique identity and historical trajectory ensure its continued sovereignty and independence.

Appendix A: Timeline of Key Events in Canadian History

This timeline highlights significant moments in Canada's history, from its colonial origins to its emergence as a sovereign nation. It provides a chronological overview of the events that have shaped Canada's identity and its relationship with the British Empire, the Commonwealth, and the United States.

-1534: Jacques Cartier claims the territory of New France for France.
-1763: The Treaty of Paris ends the Seven Years' War; France cedes most of its North American territories to Britain.
-1774: The Quebec Act guarantees French Canadians the right to practice their religion and retain their legal system.
-1791: The Constitutional Act divides Quebec into Upper Canada (English-speaking) and Lower Canada (French-speaking).

-1812–1815: The War of 1812 solidifies Canada's distinct identity and loyalty to Britain.

-1867: The British North America Act establishes the Dominion of Canada through Confederation.

-1914–1918: Canada's contributions to World War I, including the Battle of Vimy Ridge, bolster its national identity.

-1931: The Statute of Westminster grants Canada full legislative independence.

-1965: Canada adopts the maple leaf flag, symbolizing its distinct national identity.

-1982: The Constitution is patriated, and the Canadian Charter of Rights and Freedoms is enacted.

-1995: The second Quebec referendum on sovereignty results in a narrow victory for the "No" side.

-2015: The Truth and Reconciliation Commission releases its final report, calling for reconciliation with Indigenous peoples.

-2020: Canada celebrates 153 years of Confederation, reaffirming its commitment to diversity, inclusivity, and sovereignty.

Appendix B: Selected Quotes from Canadian Leaders on Independence and Sovereignty

This collection of quotes from Canadian leaders highlights the nation's commitment to sovereignty, independence, and its unique identity. These quotes reflect the values and principles that have guided Canada's development as a sovereign nation.

1. Sir John A. Macdonald (First Prime Minister of Canada)

"A British subject I was born, a British subject I will die."

Macdonald's words reflect Canada's early loyalty to the British Empire while laying the groundwork for its eventual independence.

2. Lester B. Pearson (14th Prime Minister of Canada, Nobel Peace Prize Laureate)

"The choice, however, is as clear now for nations as it was once for the individual: peace or extinction."

Pearson's emphasis on peacekeeping and multilateralism underscores Canada's role as a global mediator and advocate for peace.

3. Pierre Elliott Trudeau (15th Prime Minister of Canada)

"Canada will be a strong country when Canadians of all provinces feel at home in all parts of the country, and when they feel that all Canada belongs to them."

Trudeau's vision of a united and inclusive Canada reflects the nation's commitment to diversity and federalism.

4. Kim Campbell (19th Prime Minister of Canada)

"Canada is the homeland of equality, justice, and tolerance."

Campbell's words highlight Canada's values of inclusivity and social justice.

5. Justin Trudeau (23rd Prime Minister of Canada)

"Diversity is our strength. We are not a melting pot; we are a beautiful mosaic."

Trudeau's emphasis on multiculturalism reflects Canada's identity as a nation that celebrates diversity.

6.Louis Riel (Métis Leader and Founder of Manitoba)

"My people will sleep for one hundred years, but when they awake, it will be the artists who give them their spirit back."

Riel's words, though spoken in the context of Indigenous struggles, resonate with Canada's ongoing journey toward reconciliation and cultural renewal.

Appendix C: Further Reading and Resources

For readers interested in exploring the topics discussed in this book in greater depth, this section provides a list of recommended books, articles, and online resources.

1.Books

   - A Short History of Canada by Desmond Morton

   - The Idea of Canada: Letters to a Nation by David Johnston

   - Peacekeeping: The Canadian Way by J.L. Granatstein

   - Indigenous Writes: A Guide to First Nations, Métis, and Inuit Issues in Canada by Chelsea Vowel

2.Articles and Reports

   - Truth and Reconciliation Commission of Canada: Calls to Action (2015)

   - The Canadian Encyclopedia (online resource)

- Canada's Role in the World: A Historical Perspective by John English

3. Online Resources

   - Government of Canada's official website:

www.canada.ca

   - The Commonwealth's official website:

www.thecommonwealth.org

   - Canadian Museum of History:

www.historymuseum.ca

www.ingramcontent.com/pod-product-compliance
Lightning Source LLC
Chambersburg PA
CBHW071722020426
42333CB00017B/2357